KNOW ABOUT
RABINDRANATH TAGORE

MAPLE KIDS

KNOW ABOUT RABINDRANATH TAGORE

Published by

MAPLE PRESS PRIVATE LIMITED
office: A-63, Sector 58, Noida 201301, U.P., India
phone: +91 120 455 3581, 455 3583
email: info@maplepress.co.in
website: www.maplepress.co.in

Reprinted in 2019

ISBN: 978-93-50334-10-2

Contents

Preface

Gurudev Rabindranath Tagore is probably one of the most widely read of the poets of Bengal. In fact, he is the only poet that Bengal actually worships. For the people of India and abroad, he was the very soul of Indian culture and the living voice of India.

The literary life of the 'Voice of India', which extended over sixty years, is marked with abundance and variety, which reminds one of Victor Hugo the French poet, novelist, and dramatist and one of the world famous writers. He wrote over one thousand poems, nearly two dozen plays and playlets, eight novels, more than eight volumes of short stories, more than two thousand songs, of which he wrote the lyrics as well as composed the music; and a mass of prose on literary, social, religious, political and other topics. Apart from these there are also his English translations, paintings, travels and lecture-tours in Asia, America and Europe. Rabindranath Tagore made remarkable contributions to the society as an educationist, a social and religious reformer, and a politician, this made the genius one of the most prominent figures of not just Indian, but World history. One of his excellent biography describes that, he was a myriad-minded man – the kind of figure a nation probably gets only once in its life.

CHAPTER 1
Early Years

Rabindranath Tagore was born on May 7, 1861, in Kolkata. He was the youngest of the fourteen children of Maharshi Debendranath Tagore (a leader of the Brahmo Samaj) and Sarada Devi. The Tagores were cultured and wealthy family. Tagore's grandfather, Dwarkanath Tagore had established a huge financial kingdom through investment and speculation in coal mines, indigo, and sugar. He had helped many public works, one such contribution was the Calcutta Medical College. The Tagores lived in a joint family in Jorasanko. Tagore belonged to a family of poets, scholars, philosophers, artists, musicians and freedom fighters. The family name was actually Thakur, Tagore is its English version. In *My Reminiscences*, Tagore writes that he used socks and shoes at the age of ten.

Tagore spent most of his early life in an atmosphere of religion, arts, literature, music and painting. In religion, the Vedas and the Upanishads influenced him. Tagore's musical training was in Indian classical music. He also had training in European music during his first visit to

England and some of his early songs were composed to the tunes of the *Border Ballads* and Moore's *Irish Melodies*. But most of his musical compositions came from Bengali folk music of the *Baul* and *Bhatiyali type*.

Rabindranath Tagore was very sure that he would be a writer. He was brought up on three languages, Sanskrit, Bengali and English.

The most influencing were the Sanskrit classics. The *Vaisnava* poets of Bengal and the English romantics and post-romantics also influenced him. He grew up in the lap of nature, learning to love and worship it.

The Tagores tried to mix up traditional Indian culture with Western ideas. It is to be mentioned here that all the children contributed a lot to Bengali literature and culture. Rabi, as Rabindranath was called in his childhood and younger days, started to compose poems at the age of seven. Tagore's first book, a collection of poems, appeared when he was only 17. The book was published by one of Tagore's close friends to give him a surprise.

CHAPTER 2
Education

In 1868, at the age of seven, Tagore was admitted into the Oriental Seminary. He cleared his first examination with distinction and got first position in Bengali. During this time, he got his first lessons in composing poems from Jyotiprakash, grandson of Girindranath. Though Tagore enjoyed these lessons very much, yet for the young Tagore, school and classroom was a bar with four walls. In those days of pre-independence, special arrangements were made for taking lessons in English. These lessons were held in the evening. Tagore used to hate those classes and felt that the birds were luckier than him, as they are not bound to study like he have to do.

His dislikes during this time was expressed best in the first poem he wrote, which reads as follows:

I do not aspire to study and be learned
or be wise and a good boy as you wish
I would rather play always and wander about
to search for the corvine in the Mulberry bush.

When I hear the cart-driver's song,

to cross the vast fields, he drives fast,

I cannot learn my lessons any long

And promise to become a literate at last.

Tagore found lessons in the school very dull and hated

the idea of physical punishment, like other well-known people such as Mahatma Gandhi. Soon, Tagore was sent to a regular school and after that to St. Xavier's.

In spite of growing up in luxury, Tagore used his long creative life to understand, sympathize and defend the history, culture of the common people of India. He believed that India needs to be free from the hold of Britishers and this has been expressed perfectly in his writings.

CHAPTER 3
The Growing Poet

Debendranath Tagore (Rabi's father) used to spend most of his days in the Himalayas. When Rabi was twelve years old, his father came home for Rabi's sacred thread ceremony, which is a custom still popular among the brahmins of India. Thereafter, Debendranath took Rabi with him to spend a few months in the Himalayas.

During their journey towards the hills, they spend a few days at Santiniketan Ashram (a retreat in rural Bengal founded by Debendranath in 1863), where his father had built a garden house to spend time in meditation. The stay at Santiniketan influenced young Rabi's mind and played an important role in shaping his future life.

This journey disciplined him and taught him many things. He learnt Sanskrit from his father, moved around freely in the mountains and forests. This trip brought a change in his character as a growing poet. His father also encouraged him to develop self-discipline, independence of spirit and dislike controlling behaviour.

In 1875, when Tagore was only fourteen years old, his mother passed away. This was the first time that he saw death from very close. Her death taught him the truth of life. Deeply affected by this great loss, he became very thoughtful. He realized that in life everything was closely woven between laughter and tear. Nothing more could be seen beyond this, hence he accepted this as the ultimate.

He reached out to his sister-in-law (his elder brother's wife), Kadambari, for support. Tagore and Kadambari were about the same age. As the mother's instinct comes early to women, Kadambari filled up the emptiness in Tagore's life after the death of his mother. After the tragedy, she always kept guarding Rabi, even when she would move from place to place away from their ancestor's house. To this young brother-in-law of her own age, she had extended great affection and love. She was a highly gifted lady. She not only loved literature, but also took keen interest in it, particularly in poetry. She encouraged the poetic talent of her brother-in-law, Rabi. She proved to be Rabi's guardian angel who replaced his mother and also became his playmate, the company he wanted the most in the critical period of his boyhood. It was she who introduced Biharilal, the first lyric-poet in Bengal to Rabi. She also liked Bankim Chandra Chatterjee's writings. She would ask Rabi to read them for her. Thus a warm friendship and love grew between young Rabindranath and Kadambari Devi. One of the famous biographers of Rabindranath, described this love as, "Too deep and sacred to be categorized in terms of normal human relationship."

During this time, Tagore wrote a patriotic poem, which was published in the *Amrit Bazar Patrika*.

CHAPTER 4
In England and Marriage

In 1878, when Rabindranath was seventeen years old, his elder brother Satyendranath expressed his wish to go to the United Kingdom to prepare himself for the Bar. Satyendranath who was the first Indian member of the Indian Civil Service, to England. He also requested his father's permission to take young Rabi along with him. Father gave his permission and the two brothers sailed for England in the same year.

During his stay of three years, Rabi studied English literature at the London University under the guidance of Prof. Henry Morley and had many experiences, which he described in his long letters that he wrote to his father at home. During this time Rabindra wrote his first book of Poetry, *Sandhya Sangeet*. During the short stay in London, Tagore gathered good knowledge of Western music. The Western music that attracted him the most was the romantic ones. While in England, he also wrote a poem, *Bhanga Hriday*, in which he described about the sufferings of a broken heart away from home.

But, soon his father called him back and as a result he had to return to India in 1880, before completing any educational qualification. This turn of events took place due to his father's growing worry on Rabindranath's liking for white women and English life.

After returning to India in 1880, he wrote two verse plays in Bengali, entitled 'Valmiki Pratibha' and 'Kaal Mryigaya'.

On December 9, 1883, he married Bhabatarini, the daughter of Benimadhav Chowdhury. She was at the time just ten years old, quite thin, not at all good-looking

and semi literate. But, Rabi accepted his father's choice without even meeting her. The wedding took place at the family home Jorasanko. After the marriage, Bhabatarini was renamed as Mrinalini by Rabindranath.

CHAPTER 5
Santiniketan

Before Rabindranath's second trip to England for further studies during 1878, he was sent to Bombay to stay with Dr. Atmaram Pandurang Turkhud family. He was an eminent physician and founder of the Prarthana Sabha, also was a good friend of Rabi's elder brother Satyendranath. Annapurna Turkhud (Ana) was made mentor of Rabi to improve his felicity with English language and to help imbide the English mannerisms. Ana was the daughter of Dr. Turkhud who had just returned from England and was conversant with the nicest of the English culture and the language. A warm and affectionate relationship developed between them during the mentoring period. Ana encouraged and inspired him remarkably. Inspired by her, he wrote a poem on her and gave her the name, *Nalini*.

In 1887, *Rajarishi* was published. The year 1889 brought the publication of Tagore's first novel, *Raja O Rani*.

The period from 1890 to 1900 was the time when Tagore's literary intelligence was at full bloom. It was during these years that he wrote the best of his works like *Manasi, Sonar Tari, Chaitali, Kshanika, Kalpana and Kadi O Komal.* Most of his works were written in Bengali. And the majority of his works suggests his support for feminism. He was a strict supporter of widow remarriage and the upliftment of women. His works gave a sight of the conditions of women during those times.

When Tagore was twenty-two, Kadambari Devi, the beloved sister-in-law, committed suicide. This created emptiness in his life and he felt very lonely. She was his best friend who stood by him during the most difficult times of his youth and now she was no more. Her death made him sensitive and his works became deep and improved. The depth of his grief was expressed again and again in his poetry *Tumi Ki Kebuli Chhabi* (Are you only

a portrait?). She lives on, immortalized through the poet's words, through his writing, and through his works of art.

In 1898, Rabindranath with his wife and five children (three daughters and two sons), shifted to his estate house in Shealdah. Due to his worst experiences at school, Tagore decided to educate his children himself. He also planned to start a school different from the normal schools.

He decided to start a school at Santiniketan where he had been with his father. On December 22, 1901, Rabindranath started the school at Santiniketan with five pupils and five teachers. It was devoted to Indian and Western values and education, this was what he wanted to achieve all his life. This was because in India he had to defend Western thought and outside he had to defend Indian thoughts. *Santiniketan* later became a university and was renamed *Vishwa Bharati.*

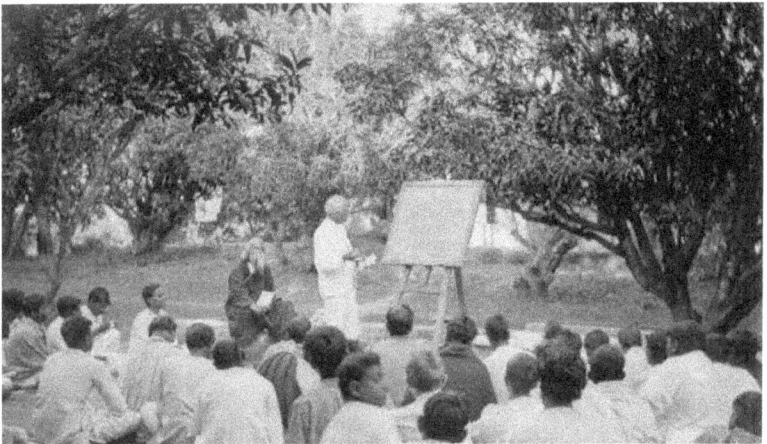

CHAPTER 6
The Rough Years

These years were the most tiring years in the life of Rabindranath Tagore because after losing his guardian angel, Kadambari Devi, Tagore also lost both his elder brother and his father.

All of a sudden, Mrinalini Devi, his wife fell ill and was brought to Calcutta. In 1902, she was brought to Jorasanko from Santiniketan but the doctors were not able to identify her illness. She could not recover and breathed her last breathe in November 23, 1902. Her death broke down Tagore and his heart. He poured his feelings out in a series of poems.

Mrinalini was not even thirty when she died. She died within months after her eldest daughter Madhurilata, nicknamed Bela, was married. Mrinalini left behind three daughters and two sons. The eldest was fifteen and the youngest was seven and so the upbringing of the remaining children fell into Rabindranath's hands.

Rabindranath shared a very loving relationship with his wife Mrinalini. She loved him so deeply that to please him she learned Bengali, English and Sanskrit. She even translated a short version of the *Ramayana* to Bengali from Sanskrit. The love she received from her husband in return too was precious.

When she was on her sick bed, Tagore would wave a hand-fan over her night after night, although she requested him to take rest. Most of Rabindranath's poetry shows how Mrinalini's death reveals the mysteries of life. However, the cruel game of fate was not yet over. Deaths of many more of his loved ones were to follow.

Months after this, his second daughter Renuka became seriously ill. Her sickness was identified as tuberculosis.

He tried to save her life. But, she passed away after a few days of her mother's death in September 1903.

Although she had been ill yet she was full of life and restlessness. The few happy moments both father and daughter had on their way to a health resort inside a train, was seen in the poem *Phanki* (Deception) in *Palataka* which read as follows;

When treatment for a year and a half wore out her bones
Then they said, 'needs change of air'.

CHAPTER 7
Deaths

In 1907, Tagore's youngest son of thirteen years, Shamindranath, had gone to Munger, also known as Monghyr, on a trip with a friend. There, Shamindranath was attacked with Cholera. Tagore received a telegram from his son and immediately left Calcutta for Munger. Shamindra passed away on the same date as his mother had expired five years before.

Rabindranath wrote in a letter,

"What you have heard is not incorrect. Bhola had gone to Munger to his maternal uncle's; Shami, too, went with him; he never returned."

Some years later, Rabindranath wrote a poem in memory of his son, which had the lines,

"When Biju went away to that world beyond death,

Cutting away the many bonds of his father-

It felt as though the dawn in my room had died from a bursting heart."

After a few days his eldest child, daughter Madhurilata, was affected by tuberculosis as well. Madhurilata's husband was not on good terms with the Tagores. At midday, Rabindranath would travel in a covered coach to visit his daughter. His son-in-law would be in the court at that time. All afternoon, he would narrate stories to his daughter or read her poems. Perhaps, one or two of these have found their way into his *Palataka's 'Mukti'*.

One afternoon, as he arrived in front of the house, he heard the sound of weeping from inside. The poet immediately ordered the coachman to return back. He did not enter the house, though he wept remembering his daughter, who would always wait for his poems.

At this time, he understood that his wife, son, daughters, all escaped much before their time. They were all fugitives (*escapee*). Hence, months after Madhurilata's death, the collection '*The fugitives*' came out. In this book, there is an unforgettable mark of Madhuri, Renuka and Shami.

In Palataka's last poem, *Shesh Pratishtha* (Last Foundation), Tagore wrote,

I hear this often, 'Is gone, is gone'
Yes say I this
do not say 'Is not.'...
There I wish to immerse my Life
In the ocean where 'Is' and 'Is Not' fulfilled remain equal.

This poem was for all fugitives.

After all the fugitives had escaped, the poet was left with only his son Rathindranath and daughter Mira. Mira had a son and a daughter.

Rabindranath was very loving towards his grandson, Nitu. Often, he would dress the little child in a fine *dhoti and kurta*. Nitu went to Europe, but he died there of tuberculosis at nineteen or twenty. At that time, the poet was seventy-one.

These situations in the life of the poet, no doubt, played an important role in the making of Tagore, the writer and the man.

CHAPTER 8
The Patriot

In 1905, when Bengal was partitioned, Tagore was filled with patriotism. Though he was in the beginning a supporter of Gandhi yet he could not accept his ideology and kept himself away from politics. In fact, it was Gandhi, who had given him the title *Gurudev*. Gandhi often talked with Tagore to discuss the methods that are to be used to gain freedom for India.

Jawaharlal Nehru once said for Tagore and Gandhiji that; both of them followed many ideas from West and other countries. But they did this for the world. They were true sons of India and followed the same old culture yet they differ a lot from each other.

Though personal sufferings left Tagore heartbroken yet he did not spend time in grief. Instead, he poured out all his sorrow into his writings and devoted his energies to various reforms and nationalist activities. Gitanjali, his masterpiece, was born out of this loss. Gitanjali (Song of offerings), the book on which Rabindranath Tagore won

the Nobel Prize was the first book of English translation of his poems. Gitanjali was a collection of hundred and three poems, translated by the poet from his various poetical works in Bengali. The Westerners considered his work to be the best literary production of the year in the whole world.

His father gave Tagore his political ideals. He used his literature to organize social and political reforms. His patriotic songs were the call for freedom and waking up to fight for freedom. He wrote the lyrics of *Jana Gana Mana*, which was later declared the National Anthem of India. He also wrote the National Anthem of Bangladesh "*Amar Sonar Bangla*". He was a nationalist and a patriot like his father. But, above all, he was a poet, the man who dreamt and inspired faith. He was a strict believer of freedom for India.

In 1919, the British Government honoured Tagore with Knighthood, presenting him the title 'Sir'. But, Tagore refused to accept the knighthood after the massacre at the Jallianwallah Bagh, which shocked and angered him a lot. In fact, he wrote a letter to the Viceroy, expressing his anger on such an inhuman act.

CHAPTER 9
Ideas for Santiniketan

Rabindranath was a true nationalist and this was displayed in his personal life as well. Tagore wanted his son to gain scientific knowledge in order to solve the problem of food shortage in India. With this aim in mind, Tagore sent his eldest son Rathindranath, and Santosh Chandra, son of a friend, to study agriculture and animal farming in the United States in 1905. At that time, Rathindranath was seventeen and Santosh was eighteen years old. In those days, it was common for the sons of rich families to travel abroad, particularly England, to study law or prepare for Civil Service by completing the I.C.S (Indian Civil Service) examinations.

Sometime later, Rabindranath sent his youngest son-in-law, Nagendranath Gangopadhyay, to the United States for the same purpose. It was extremely rare in those days to choose the United States for higher studies over England, Germany, France or Japan. Rathindranath has described in his *Pitrismriti* and *On the Edges of Time* that no one from the University of Illinois was present to receive him at the railway station because they had supposed that two students were due to arrive from Indiana instead of India.

Tagore travelled to the United States for the first time by the end of 1912, together with Rathindranath and his daughter-in-law, Pratima Devi. Even though he was then over fifty, his name was hardly known in the West. From New York, they travelled to Urbana, the small town where Rathindranath had studied at the university. This time, Rathindranath began to study biology.

After spending six months at United States, the poet grew tired mentally. It had been planned at the beginning

that they would stay there for a while and Rathindranath would finish his research in the meantime. The chief outcome of this trip was a major change in Tagore's view for the Brahmacharya Ashram at Santiniketan. He felt the need of a technical division and a hospital there and educate the students in science. He thought that Jagadananda Roy, a science teacher and writer of popular science, and Rathindranath would carry out research in the laboratories. By this time, the poet was also developing the idea of creating a university at Santiniketan.

CHAPTER 10
Gitanjali and Vishwa Bharati

Tagore's reputation as a writer was established in the United States and in England only after the publication of *Gitanjali: Song Offerings*, in which he gave voice to God and human love. The poems were translated into English by the author himself.

Tagore's poems were also praised by Ezra Pound and it drew the attention of the Nobel Prize committee. Ezra Pound once mentioned in *The Fortnightly Review* that; there is in him the stillness of nature. The poems do not seem to have been produced by storm or by ignition, but seem to show the normal habit of his mind *Gitanjali*, within a year of its translation, shacked Europe and earned him name and fame. *Gitanjali* is a book of spiritual lyrics with supreme beauty. Tagore experimented with poetic forms and all were translated into other languages. He was awarded the Nobel Prize for it and became the first Indian to a Noble Prize. With the help of the money he got from the Nobel Prize he established Santiniketan.

In 1924, he introduced the *Vishwa Bharati* University at Santiniketan. This was his effort of mixing the Indian and Western methods of education. He is remembered much for Santiniketan than his literary excellence. In the years that followed, Rabindranath went on to become one of the most formidable literary forces India has ever produced. As one of the earliest educators to think in terms of the global village, he envisioned an education that was deeply rooted in one's immediate surroundings but connected to the cultures of the wider world.

Tagore now decided to materialize his dream university. But had no money for it and taking (British) government's money for his work at Santiniketan might block his freedom. To run a university at Santiniketan he worked very hard for the rest of his life to raise the funds by earning from his works within and outside India. Unfortunately, he faced acute financial miseries always.

Fortunately, in 1916, Major J. B. Pond of the Lyceum proposed to Tagore that he would receive $12,000 if he agreed to present lectures at several U.S. cities according to a schedule prepared by his organization. On account of the Nobel Prize he received for his work and also that many of his writings were by then been translated into several European languages, Rabindranath was at this time an internationally famous figure. On his trip Tagore was accompanied by, C. F. Andrews, William Pearson and Mukul De, a young painter. Beginning with Seattle,

Rabindranath travelled across the United States giving lectures in different cities.

In a letter written during that tour, he wrote (to paraphrase a delightfully rhyming *bon mot*),

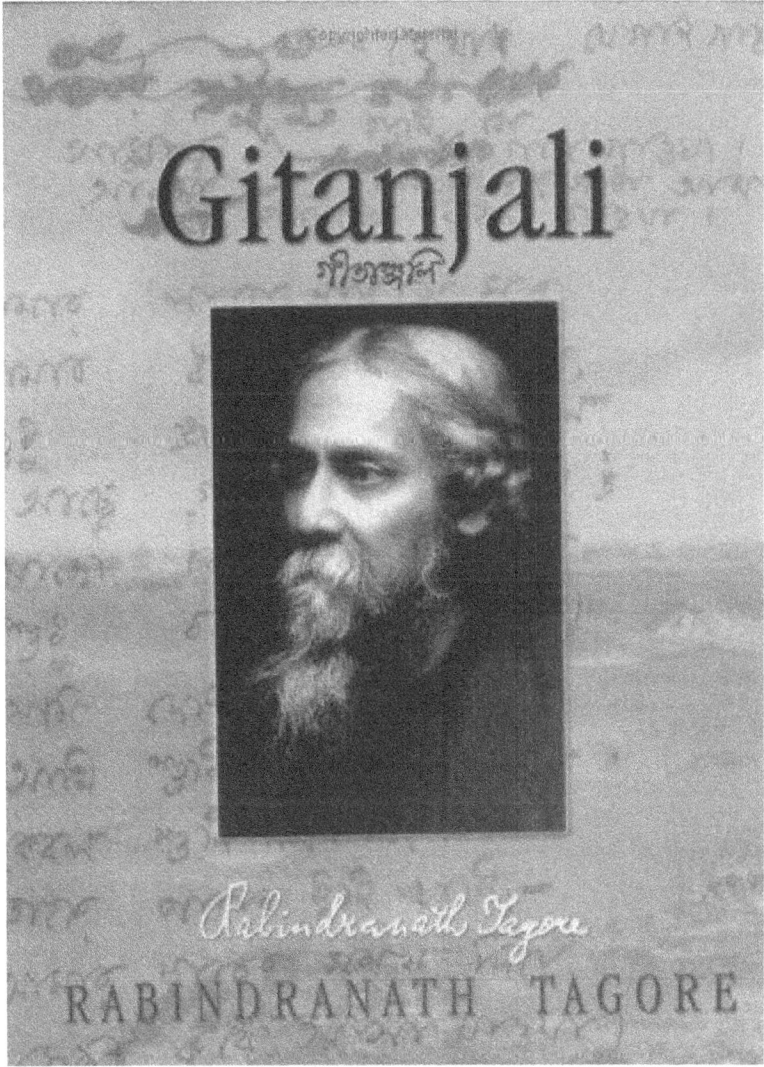

"I travel, I roar, I earn, I dissipate."

But due to some reasons Rabindranath was forced to cancel his contract, although he had a huge financial loss. The lectures he presented on the tour were found in his books *Nationalism* and *Personality*. At the time of the tour, Europe was engaged in World War I. He repeatedly warned that the spirit of nationalism would drag the world towards destruction and encouraged self-control and alertness. Many people in Europe and America were greatly irritated by Tagore's anti-nationalist message. This was the main reason why Tagore was not popular in the West. After arriving in New York on a tour of the United States in the year 1920, Tagore saw that the interest with which he was received during his former visit was lacking a lot. He gave a few lectures in New York and at Harvard, there was no respect and warmth around him. This time also his efforts of fund-raising for *Vishwa Bharati* ended with dissatisfaction. No one paid any attention to his message about India's 'mystic' poet and showed no interest in knowing about *Vishwa Bharati*.

CHAPTER 11
His Tours

Tagore received an invitation from the Junior League after a few months in 1920. However, here, too, he was unsuccessful in raising any money. One professor wanted to know the British government's attitude towards *Santiniketan*. It gradually became clear to Rabindranath that his surrender of the Knighthood in 1919 in protest of the Amritsar massacre did not please the Americans also. But positively, the American Poetry Society gave him a warm reception.

At the same time, Major Pond of the Lyceum had arranged for fifteen lectures in Texas. During this lecture tour, Rabindranath met Leonard Elmhirst for the first time. This young Englishman later helped Rabindranath in his rural development project at Sriniketan, a village near Santiniketan. He accompanied Tagore on his journey to South America in 1924, and when Tagore fell ill on the ship, he took care of him for two months in Argentina. Elmhirst's American friend, Dorothy Straight, who later became his wife, provided funds for the work at Sriniketan.

Overall, Tagore received very little fund from this tour of the United States.

In 1929, Canada's Council of Education invited Tagore to discuss his ideas on Education and Leisure. This was his first formal approval as an educator from India. In Vancouver, he met Canada's Governor General, Lord Willingdon, who later became the Viceroy of India.

During the tour of 1929, Rabindranath received invitations from several U.S. cities, and finally arrived at Los Angeles. An encounter with the immigration officials at the port of entry offended Tagore a lot.

Thus, he decided to go to Japan instead. But he was detained for several hours by the U.S. customs.

After his tour of the Soviet Union, Tagore returned to the U.S. in late 1930. One of the business organizations

in U.S. welcomed him at a grand dinner reception (with 500 invited guests). Commenting on the reception, the *Saturday Review noted* that there were several well-known business and wealthy persons listed among the invitees but there was no recognizable writer or poet among them.

Rabindranath had a meeting with President Herbert Hoover, arranged by the Ambassador of Great Britain. There were several exhibitions of his paintings but no lectures were organized. Once again, his hopes of raising funds for education, in the U.S., were shattered.

CHAPTER 12
In South America

In May 1924, Rabindranath Tagore received an invitation to participate in the celebration of the anniversary of Peru's independence in December of that year. In September, he boarded the ship *Haruna Maru*, which was bound for Europe, at Colombo. During the passage from France to South America on Ship *Andes*, he fell ill.

In a letter to C. F. Andrews, he later wrote, "...On October 24, I had written a poem addressed to the '*Terrible*' (the two poems, *Jhar* and *Padadhwani*, written on that day appears in the collection *Purabi*). Since that day, I have suffered so much that I thought I was going to die. When I came to Buenos Aires, the doctor's advice prevented my proceeding to Peru."

Tagore arrived in Buenos Aires on November 7, 1924, only a few days after an essay called, T*he joy of Reading Tagore* in the magazine *La Nacion* was published by a lady called Victoria Ocampo. This lady was greatly moved by Tagore's *Gitanjali* and later became a very good friend of the poet. Born in 1890 into an aristocratic Argentinean family, she was married in 1912, and was divorced in 1922. To free herself from loneliness, she started to read her favourite writer's works. She translated many famous writings from French and English literature to Argentine.

In Buenos, Leonard Elmhirst was Tagore's secretary. The doctors had advised him to cancel his plan to cross the Andes and go to Lima. They told him to rest for some days in the countryside till he gets well to board another ship.

After learning about this Victoria asked Elmhirst to take Rabindranath to San Isidro, a suburb about 20 miles from Buenos Aires and spend a few days there. She rented a garden house from a relative for Tagore to live in. From

its roof and the hall on the second floor, one could see the river. The garden was full of flowers.

Victoria's first meeting with Tagore was brief, but it delighted and impressed her a lot. Tagore spent almost two months in the garden house in San Isidro.

The poet would spend his mornings writing, walking in the garden, or reading. During the evenings, he was surrounded by visitors and admirers. Once in a while, he would even get unexpected visitors, such as a woman who came in to ask the poet to explain her dreams.

CHAPTER 13
Victoria Ocampo

Tagore called Victoria Ocampo by the Bengali name equal to her as, *Bijaya*. He dedicated his collection *Purabi*, which was published in 1925, to *The Lotus Palms* of *Bijaya*. Thirty poems in this collection were written in San Isidro. Tagore had composed around 400 poems on love and nature. Many of them came after meeting Ocampo. "*Puravi*" contains all the poems that Tagore had composed with Victoria in mind. "The gifts exchanged between the two encapsulate the intensity of Tagore's and Ocampo's feelings for each other, the desire for each other's company. It was a deeply spiritual and emotional association, and each of them was influenced by the other."

It was *Bijaya*, who first encouraged Tagore to paint. In 1924, while writing "*Purabi*," Tagore started "doodling" on the pages of his manuscript – crossing out lines that he did not like and turning them into forms and shapes. Rabindranath creatively used his lack of formal training in art by experimenting new horizons in the use of line and color. He would delete unwanted words or even whole lines by creating strange intriguing images so that the whole page became a work of art. Victoria took photographs of these work. Six years later when she met him in Paris,

she along with her friend arranged an exhibition at the *Gallerie Pigalle*.

It was Bijaya who paid for all the arrangements of the exhibition. The exhibition later moved on to London, Birmingham and Berlin. Several stars of the art world, including Riviere, Kollwitz and Noailles praised the paintings for their originality.

CHAPTER 14
Victoria and Tagore

Victoria's Latin American involvement helped Tagore with his poetry. In a letter to Rani Chanda, Tagore wrote that Bijaya always discussed many subjects with him but he did not know Spanish and it was difficult for her to explain him in English too. He took regretted of not learning languages and it was due to this barrier Tagore's was unable to adjust to the Latin culture.

In his poem

Exotic Blossom, he wrote,

"Exotic Blossom, I whispered again in your ear

What is your language, dear?

You smiled and shook your head

And the leaves murmured instead."

Tagore had written the song, in 1895, *Ami Chini Go Chini Tomare, Ogo Bideshini* (I know you well, O exotic woman, I know you well) while he was in Shealdah. He had given Bijaya a translation of the song within days after they had first met. There are only two poems in which

Tagore had directly addressed Bijaya. The first, which appears in Purabi under the title *Atithi* (The Guest), begins with the lines, *The days of my sojourn overseas, you filled to the fullest, woman, with the nectar of your sweetness...* The second, written in April 1941, only months before his death, appears as the fifth poem in Shesh Lekha (The Last Words). It reads,

With love so earnest and extrinsic

The beloved who found a place in my heart

Forever shall keep me bound

The words she whispered, though oceans apart.

Her language I knew not

Her eyes that spoke a language of their own

Forever shall awaken in my mind

Their plaintive message, though unknown.

The relation between Tagore and Bijaya continued for fifteen years in the form of letters. Most of these are now kept properly in the Rabindra Sadan. Towards the end of his life, this Argentinean poetess influenced Tagore a lot. Unfortunately, Victoria Ocampo could never visit India because of her poor health and other situations. She wrote a short book about Tagore and translated his play, *Rakta Karabi* (Red Oleanders) into Spanish. As editor of the literary magazine *Sur* and as a poetess, she received much honour in South America. Victoria Ocampo died in January 27, 1979.

The ties between India and Latin America are still weak, yet Tagore is a familiar and honourable name for the educated Latin American circles till today.

On his way back to India, Tagore had stopped for a day in Rio de Janeiro. Cecilia Meireles, a famous Brazilian poetess has to her credit one of the finest translations of Tagore's poetry into Portuguese. Rabindranath Tagore is the first known poetry connection between India and Brazil. There is even a school named after Tagore in Rio de Janeiro.

CHAPTER 15
Last Phase of Life

Rabindranath traveled to over 30 countries on five continents in a little over five decades in the late 19th century and the early 20th century. Later in 1913 after he had won the Nobel Prize, traveling became a part of his life. During his later years, Tagore travelled a lot.

Rabindranath Tagore met several well known people over the years. In Italy he met Benito Mussolini in Rome and soon visited Iran on the personal request by the Shah of Iran, Reza Shah Pahlavi. Soon after, he interacted with more than a bunch of world influencers like the Irish playwright George Bernard Shaw, French novelist Romain Rolland, Paul Thomas Mann a German essayist and novelist, Robert Lee Frost a poet and Dr Karel Hujer an astronomer from America and German physicist Albert Einstein among many others. He also went to England and became friends with W. B. Yeats and many other renowned people of literary intellect and they exchanged ideas. Tagore's works were widely translated into English, Dutch, German, Spanish, and other European languages.

His works, especially *Gitanjali*, was being read all over the world during that time.

By 1941, his health gave up and he was bedridden. Lying in sickbed he wrote a poem *Rogasajyay*, here he compared his state to dried sticks, which form a tiny island in the middle of a river, keeping itself, away from the main flow.

Those who attended him was shocked with his capacity of bearing pain without showing it.

The last three months of his life were filled with sufferings. In the middle of this suffering also his thoughts would wander to his beloved Santiniketan and the little children in the school. A dog used to seek shelter under his moving chair. The poet used to pet his head with his hand. One of the poems of *Arogya* is on this nameless dog. Later, when his condition grew worse he had to remain in bed and could no longer sit on the chair, he expressed his sorrow in a poem. This chair was very dear to him and he had spent many happy hours sitting in it and creating many works, at San Isidro as the guest of Victoria Ocampo. Seeing how relaxed he felt sitting in the chair, she forced him to take the chair with him when he sailed from Buenos Aires.

Tagore avoided leaving Santiniketan. The doctors asked him to undertake the operation and on the very morning when he was to be operated, Rabindranath created his last poem.

But, he never recovered from the operation. Gradually his condition worsened. On August 7, 1941, he died, at *Jorasanko*. Thousands of residents came in to pay their homage to the great poet who had woken their hearts & souls. His body was cremated on the banks of the Hoogly River.

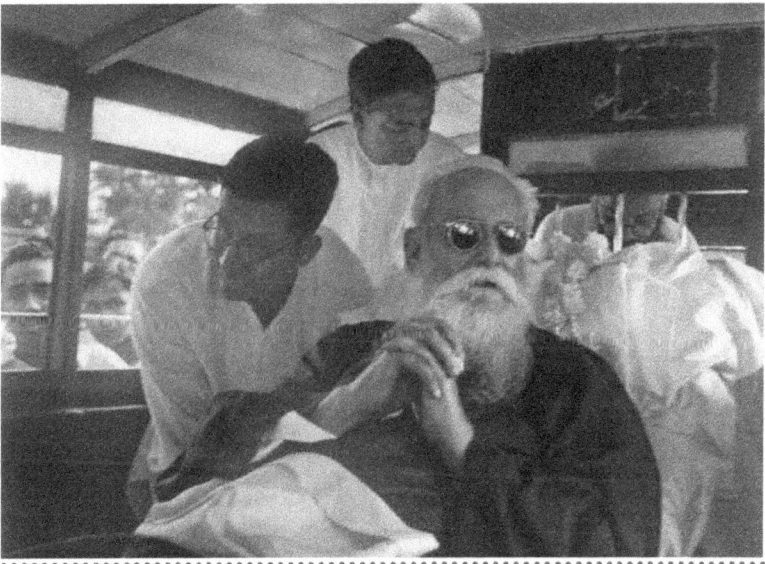

CHAPTER 16
Life Story

Tagore and Einstein

One of Tagore's most memorable meetings was that with Albert Einstein that took place in 1930. Tagore met him through a common friend, Dr. Mendel. They met each other in Berlin and in New York. Their discussions were published and are even today read with interest by anyone interested in the nature of science and philosophy.

They discussed about the scientific view of the universe and the nature of truth and beauty.

Tagore and H. G. Wells

Tagore met many geniuses and his discussion with many of them has been recorded. Some have appeared in newspapers and in books. He also met H. G. Wells in Geneva in 1930. Wells and Tagore discussed about human civilization. Another important meeting was between Hellen Keller, the blind writer and Tagore.

CHAPTER 17
Basis of Tagore's works

Tagore's ideology came from the teaching of the *Upanishads* and from his own beliefs that God can be found through sincerity and service to others. He stressed that world must follow the multinational views and ideas. He believed that the soil keeps the tree tied to her and the sky leaves it free. From his journey to Japan in 1916, he produced many articles and books.

In 1927, he embarked Southeast Asian tour and inspired many with his wisdom and literary work. *Letters from Java*, which first was serially arranged in *Vichitra*, was published as a book, *Jatri*, in 1929. His Majesty Riza Shah Pahlavi invited Tagore to Iran in 1932. On his journeys and lecture tours, Tagore tried to spread the ideology of uniting the East and the West. While in Japan, he wrote, "The Japanese do not waste their energy in useless screaming and quarrelling, and because there is no waste of energy, there is no scarcity of it. This calmness and courage of body and mind is part of their national understanding."

Tagore wrote his most important works in Bengali, but he often translated his poems into English.

Whatever Tagore wrote it marked an effect in reader's heart. He received from his father a deep love for nature which reflected in his works. He was much in love with nature and felt that he was a part of it.

Between 1893 and 1900, he wrote seven volumes of poetry. This was a highly productive period in Tagore's life and he was named as, *The Bengali Shelley*.

Tagore wrote in the common language of the people. This was hard for critics and scholars to accept it. Tagore was the first Indian to write motivating novels.

CHAPTER 18
His Writings

Tagore produced works of untold topics. Below is given some of his selected works with a brief summary.

The first book of poetry by Tagore was Sandhya Sangeet. He has expressed romantic feelings in his work beautifully. *Sandhya Sangeet* is an excellent lyric that unfolds the promising poetic career of Tagore.

Another masterpiece of his poetic creation was, *Prabhat Sangeet*, that reflects the mystic thoughts of the poet.

His next creation was *Manasi* (The Lady of the Mind). The time when he wrote this book, mankind was his subject. He turned his eyes from the beauties of the outside world to the beauty of the inner world. It expressed his anger for giving short life. Rabindranath was quite unhappy of the incomplete relation with the world and nature.

His poem *Sonar Tari* (The Golden Boat) published in 1894, is one of the most celebrated collection of poems of Rabindranath Tagore. This was the result of

Tagore's intensity of expression and mysticism. This poem describes, the poet sits "sad and alone on the bare riverbank, sheaves of cut paddy waiting beside him. A boat approaches steered by a mysterious figure, who agrees to load the paddy". The person on the bank parts with it all and then asks to be taken on board too. But there is no

room says the boatman with a smile and leaves. The poet was left standing alone on the bank of the river.

In *Chitra*, the play adapts part of the story from the *Mahabharata* and centers upon the character of Chitrangada, a female warrior who tries to attract the attention of Arjuna.

His novels were centered on ordinary life. His first two novels were *Bou Thakuranir Haat* and *Rajarshi*. Both were historical stories. The emotions of the characters were perfectly reflected in his novels.

Chokher Bali was another of his successful novels in the history of Bengali writings. The novel was based on the fight between the individual and society. Through his novels, he tried to discuss social problems.

After that, he wrote *Gora*, which was a masterpiece. In this novel, he tried to hold a mirror in front of the educated middle class.

Then came his famous novel *Ghare Baire*. The novel tried to present a sensitive young mind struggling towards individual freedom.

The most melodious of his novels was *Shesher Kobita*. With this novel is considered to be a landmark in Bengali literature.

The short story is a popular form of modern literature. It is said that a good storyteller should always be expert in writing short stories.

Tagore was the first to write short stories in Bengali. Some of his short stories are *Cloud and the Sun, The Postmaster* and *Ambition*. His short stories influenced Indian literature greatly.

His other stories are *Broken Nest, The Judge* and *The letter of the Wife*.

He was a great essayist. His best essays are *Education, Medium* of *Instruction and National Society.* The essays expressed different feelings and moods. His other essays are *The Track, The Rainy Evening, The Mind* and *The Call of the Peacock.*

Besides being an essayist, a poet and novelist he was also a dramatist.

He wrote a play called *Valmiki Pratibha* in which he acted as Valmiki.

In the play *Prakriti Pratisodh* there is a fight between two different ideologies.

His other plays are *The King and the Queen, The Sacrifice* and *Malini.*

His plays are dreamy and the flow of emotions makes it romantic and melodious. Some of his symbolic dramas are *Sarodatsav, Prayaschilta, Raja, Achalayatan, Dak Ghar, Muktadhara* and *Rakta Karabi.*

Tagore also composed songs, which were light, humorous, sorrowful and that touched the heart. Tagore was very fond of music. He set many of his texts to music. Tagore's songs were devoted to God and it shows his closeness with God.

The kind of music he composed became very popular and came to be known as Rabindra Sangeet. Today, Rabindra Sangeet is a separate school of music.

Tagore-The Love Poet

Tagore was the lover of nature, lover of life, lover of death and the lover of the mystery that unites life with death. This love helped him in relating himself with nature in her varied mood and explain his universal love, sorrow & joy. The love aspect could be seen in his every writing.

The world in which he was born and grown up has changed and this can be seen in his works.

CHAPTER 19
His Great works

The following is a list of the works of Tagore.

- Kabikahini, 1878 - a poet's tale
- Sandhya Sangeet, 1882 - evening songs
- Prabhat Sangeet, 1883 - morning songs
- Bou Thakuranir Haat - 1883
- Rajarishi, 1887
- Raja O Rani, 1889 - the king and the queen/devouring love
- Visarjan, 1890 - sacrifice
- Manasi, 1890
- Yurop Prabasir Patra, 1891, 1893
- Valmiki Pratibha, 1893
- Sonar Tari, 1894 - the golden boat
- Kanika, 1900 - moments
- Katha, 1900
- Kalpana, 1900
- Naivedya, 1901

- Nashtanir, 1901 - the broken nest
- Sharan, 1902
- Binodini, 1902
- Chokher Bali, 1903 – eyesore
- Kheya, 1906
- Naukadubi, 1906 - the wreck
- Gora, 1907-09
- Saradotsava, 1908 - autumn festival
- Galpaguchchha, 1912 - a bunch of stories
- Chinnapatra, 1912
- Viday-abhisap, 1912 - the curse at farewell
- Gitanjali, 1912 - song offerings
- Jiban Smriti, 1912 - my reminiscences
- Dakghar, 1912 - post office
- The Crescent moon, 1913
- Glimpses of Bengal life, 1913
- The hungry stones and other stories, 1913
- Chitra, 1914
- Gitimalaya, 1914
- The king of the dark chamber, 1914
- The post office, 1914
- Sadhana, 1914

His Works [1916-1941]

- Ghare-baire, 1916, the home and the world
- Balaka, 1916 - a flight of swans

- Chaturanga, 1916.
- Fruit gathering, 1916
- The hungry stones, 1916
- Stray birds, 1916
- Personality, 1917
- The cycle of spring, 1917
- Sacrifice and other plays, 1917
- My reminiscence, 1917
- Nationalism, 1917
- Mashi and other stories, 1918
- Stories from Tagore, 1918
- Palataka, 1918
- Japan-Patri, 1919 - a visit to japan
- Greater India, 1921
- The Fugitive, 1921
- Creative Unity, 1921   ,
- Lipika, 1922
- Muktadhara, 1922
- Poems, 1923
- Gora, 1924
- Letters from abroad, 1924
- Red Oleanders, 1924
- GrihaPprabesh, 1925
- Broken Ties and other stories, 1925

- Rakta-Karabi, 1925 - red oleanders
- Sadhana, 1926
- Natir puja, 1926
- Letters to a friend, 1928
- Shesher Kobita, 1929 - farewell, my friend
- Mahua, 1929, the herald of spring
- Jatri, 1929
- Yogayog, 1929
- The religion of man, 1930
- The child, 1931
- Rassiar Chithi, 1931 - letters from Russia
- Patraput, 1932
- Punascha, 1932
- Mahatmahi and the depressed humanity, 1932
- Sonar Tari, 1932
- Sheaves, poems and songs- 1932
- Dui bon, 1933 - two sisters
- Chandalika, 1933
- Malancha, 1934 - the garden
- Char adhyaya, 1934 - four Chapters
- *Bithika, 1935*
- *Shesh saptak, 1935*
- *Patraput, 1936*
- *Syamali, 1936*

- *Collected poems and plays, 1936*
- *Khapchara, 1937*
- *Semjuti, 1938*
- *Prantik, 1938*
- *Prahasini, 1939*
- *Pather sancay, 1939*
- *Akaspradip, 1939*
- *Syama, 1939*
- *Nabajatak, 1940*
- *Shanai, 1940*
- *Chelebela, 1940 - my boyhood days*
- *Rogshajyay, 1940*
- *Arogya, 1941*
- *Janmadine, 1941*
- *Galpasalpa, 1941*
- *Last poems, 1941*

Where the Mind is Without Fear (from the Gitanjali)

Where the mind is without fear and the head is held high;

Where knowledge is free;

Where the world has not been broken up

Into fragments by narrow domestic walls;

Where words come out from the depth of truth;

Where tireless striving stretches its arms towards perfection;

Where the clear stream of reason has not lost its way into the dreary desert sands of dead habit;

Where the mind is led forward by thee into ever-widening thought and action-

Into that heaven of freedom, my father, let my planet awake.

Selected Poems

Leave this chanting and singing and telling of beads! Whom dost thou worship in this lonely dark corner of a temple with doors all shut? Open thine eyes and see thy God is not before thee!

He is there where the tiller is tilling the hard ground and where the pathmaker is breaking stones. He is with them in sun and in shower, and his garment is covered with dust. Put of thy holy mantle and even like him come down on the dusty soil!

Deliverance? Where is this deliverance to be found? Our master himself has joyfully taken upon him the bonds of creation; he is bound with us all for ever.

Come out of thy meditations and leave aside thy flowers and incense! What harm is there if thy clothes become tattered and stained? Meet him and stand by him in toil and in sweat of thy brow.

*The time that my journey takes is long and
the way of it long.*

*I came out on the chariot of the first gleam of light, and
pursued my voyage through the wildernesses of worlds
leaving my track on many a star and planet.*

*It is the most distant course that comes nearest to thyself,
and that training is the most intricate which leads to the
utter simplicity of a tune.*

*The traveller has to knock at every alien door to come
to his own, and one has to wander through all the outer
worlds to reach the innermost shrine at the end.*

*My eyes strayed far and wide before I shut them and said
'Here art thou!'*

*The question and the cry 'Oh, where?' melt into tears of a
thousand streams and deluge the world with the flood of
the assurance 'I am!'*

The song that I came to sing remains unsung to this day.

I have spent my days in stringing and in unstringing
my instrument.

The time has not come true, the words have not been
rightly set; only there is the agony of wishing in my heart.

The blossom has not opened; only the wind is sighing by.
I have not seen his face, nor have I listened to his voice;
only I have heard his gentle footsteps from
the road before my house.

The livelong day has passed in spreading his seat on the
floor; but the lamp has not been lit and I cannot ask him
into my house.
I live in the hope of meeting with him;
but this meeting is not yet.

My desires are many and my cry is pitiful, but ever didst thou save me by hard refusals; and this strong mercy has been wrought into my life through and through.

Day by day thou art making me worthy of the simple, great gifts that thou gavest to me unasked - this sky and the light, this body and the life and the mind - saving me from perils of overmuch desire.

There are times when I languidly linger and times when I awaken and hurry in search of my goal; but cruelly thou hidest thyself from before me.

Day by day thou art making me worthy of thy full acceptance by refusing me ever and anon, saving me from perils of weak, uncertain desire.

I am only waiting for love to give myself up at last into his hands. That is why it is so late and why I have been guilty of such omissions.

They come with their laws and their codes to bind me fast; but I evade them ever, for I am only waiting for love to give myself up at last into his hands.

People blame me and call me heedless; I doubt not they are right in their blame.

The market day is over and work is all done for the busy. Those who came to call me in vain have gone back in anger. I am only waiting for love to give myself up at last into his hands.

www.ingramcontent.com/pod-product-compliance
Lightning Source LLC
LaVergne TN
LVHW041207080426
835508LV00008B/842